DO OUR PETS GO TO HEAVEN?

A Biblically Based Book to Prepare Children and Bring Them Comfort When Losing a Pet

J.P. Sloane, D.Min., Ph.D.

AvingtonHouse
Publishing

Other Titles by Dr. J.P. Sloane
Available from AvingtonHouse Publishers:

WHAT EVERY BIBLE BELIEVER NEEDS TO KNOW ABOUT ISLAM

EXPOSING ISLAM VOLUME I:
A Simple Crash Course on Islam

EXPOSING ISLAM VOLUME II:
The Koran
Selected Sûrahs, Commentary and Bible Comparisons

THE EVIL HISTORY OF REPLACEMENT THEOLOGY
ILLUSTRATED

DO OUR PETS GO TO HEAVEN?

A Biblically Based Book to
Prepare Children and
Bring Them Comfort When Loosing a Pet

By J.P. Sloane, D.Min., Ph.D.

ISBN-13: 978-0692607848
ISBN-10: 0692607846

AvingtonHouse Publishers, Dallas

We believe that Heaven and Hell are proper nouns describing actual places and, therefore, are capitalized in this work.

Scripture quotations marked "NIV" are from the *HOLY BIBLE, NEW INTERNATIONAL VERSION*®. Copyright © 1973, 1978, 1984, by the International Bible Society. Used by permission of Zondervan Publishing House. All rights reserved.

Archaic words found in the *KING JAMES BIBLE* have been adjusted to modern terminology.

Illustrations:
Kim Hitze, Lead Artist
Staff Artist

Dedicated to all God's creatures,
great and small,
and the children who love them.

CONTENTS

DO OUR PETS GO TO HEAVEN?

Sometimes in life things happen that we don't like or understand.

One of those things is when we lose our pet that we love so very much.

Maybe it was because of an accident or our pet just got very old, and one day it reached the end of its life.

It's hard to lose someone you really love with all your heart, and it doesn't seem fair that we should lose them.

Did you know that God hears animals when they talk?[1]

He understands what they think and feel.[2]

When you pray to God, He also listens to you because He cares what YOU think and feel.[3]

God loves you so very much and when you're hurting, He wants to comfort you.[4]

Our loving God is aware of everything that happens to little boys and girls, and God is also aware of everything that happens to animals.[5]

When you look out your window and see all the birds in the trees, God is watching with you.

He even knows and cares when one of the smallest of His birds dies and falls to the ground. [6]

God doesn't make people or pets sick, and God doesn't make bad things happen to people or pets.[7]

It's just that right now we live in an imperfect world and not Heaven, which is perfect.

Things that happen in the world are not always what we want them to be, but God promises that someday, all who love Him will be with Him forever.[8]

When that wonderful time comes, there will never be any more tears or sorrows.[9]

Have you ever wondered if there are animals in Heaven? The good news is that the Bible tells us that there are animals in Heaven.[10]

That's right! It says that God has all kinds of animals and animal-like creatures living with Him in Heaven.[11]

God made animals to be our friends and live with us on earth.[12]

It was His plan for people to love animals and take care of them.

In the beginning, the Bible tells us that God made the animals to live in a beautiful garden.[13]

And then He made people to love and share that beautiful garden with all the animals.

Did you know that in that garden people and animals never died or hurt each other and only ate berries, nuts and fruits?[14]

God also promises that one day He will make a new world to be just like it was in the beginning.[15]

Girls and boys will be able to play with lions, bears, lambs and goats.[16]

Children will be able to play with every kind of animal there is.

People and animals will never scare or hurt each other ever again![17]

God also understands how important all children and their animals are.

He knows that you may have special animal friends you love.

However, right now isn't the time that our pets will be able to live with us forever.

God knows how bad you feel. It's okay to cry and feel sad when we lose them.

The Lord holds the soul of every living thing in His hand.[18]

The day will come when no one, not people and not animals, will ever be sick or hurt or leave us ever again.[19]

God will wipe away all your tears so you can be happy forever and ever.[20]

God promises you this because He loves you and He loves your pet.

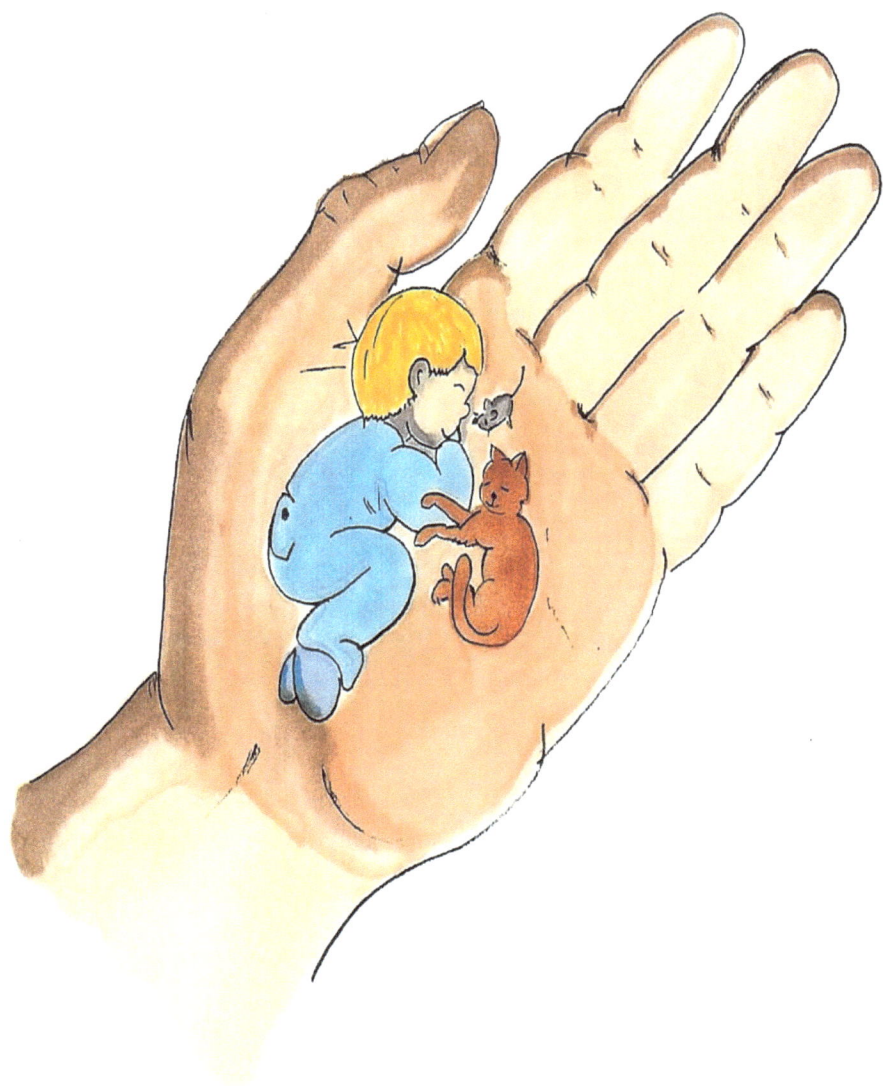

You don't have to worry about your pet anymore because the Bible says that right now, in the very throne room of God, there are angels, people and animals![21]

God tells you and me a lot about His love for us and the animals in His book, the Holy Bible.

WHAT IMPORTANT PEOPLE OF FAITH HAVE TO SHARE WITH US ABOUT OUR PETS IN HEAVEN

KING SOLOMON
(10th Century B.C.)
The Wisest Man of All Time

Solomon tells us that both people and animals have all things in common.[22] Solomon also tells us that Humans and animals have immortal spirits and asks, who can tell that it's only the spirit of people that goes to Heaven.[23] Then he tells us the answer, "...the spirit returns to God Who gave it".[24]

KING SOLOMON

MARTIN LUTHER

(1483 - 1546 A.D.)
The Father of the
Protestant Reformation

Martin Luther was overheard telling his beloved pet, "Be comforted little dog, thou too in the resurrection shall have a little golden tale!"[25]

MARTIN LUTHER

POPE JOHN PAUL II
(1920-2005 A.D.)

"Animals possess a soul and men must love and feel solidarity (unity) with our smaller brethren...."

"Animals are as near to God as men are."[26]

POPE JOHN PAUL II

JOHN WESLEY

(1703-1791 A.D.)
Founder of the
Methodist Church

"The whole animal creation will, without any doubt, be restored not only to vigor, strength and swiftness which they had when God first made them, but even more so when God gives them a perfect resurrection body."[27]

JOHN WESLEY

SAINT BASIL THE GREAT

(330-379 A.D.)
Bishop of Caesar and Founder of Monastic Institutions

"We humbly pray for the animals for which you have Thy great tenderness of heart, for Thou has promised to save (eternally) both man and animals and great is Thy loving kindness, O Master, Savior of the world."[28]

ST. BASIL THE GREAT

SAINT FRANCIS OF ASSISI
(1181-1226 A.D.)
Patron Saint of Animals and Founder of the Francian Order of Monks, Also Known as The Franciscans

"I cannot imagine Heaven without animals!"[29]

ST. FRANCIS OF ASSISI

REFERENCES

1. "Praise the LORD from the earth, you great sea creatures and all ocean depths, lightning and hail, snow and clouds, stormy winds that do His bidding, you mountains and all hills, fruit trees and all cedars, wild animals and all cattle, small creatures and flying birds" (Psalm 148:7-10, NIV).

   "Let everything that has breath [*everything* includes animals alike] praise the LORD" (Psalm 150:6, NIV, clarification mine, emphasis added).

2. God understands how animals feel. He even knew what a little donkey was thinking as he was being abused by its owner, God even made it possible for the little donkey to speak his thoughts and feelings! The story goes this way. A false prophet named:

   "Balaam got up in the morning, saddled his donkey and went with the Moabite officials. But God was very angry when he went, and the angel of the LORD stood in the road to oppose him. Balaam was riding on his donkey, and his two servants were with him. When the donkey saw the angel of the LORD standing in the road with a drawn sword in his hand, it turned off the road into a field. Balaam beat it to get it back on the road.

   "Then the angel of the LORD stood in a narrow path through the vineyards, with walls on both sides. When the donkey saw the angel of the LORD, it pressed close to the wall, crushing Balaam's foot against it. So he beat the donkey again.

   "Then the angel of the LORD moved on ahead and stood in a narrow place where there was no room to turn, either to the right or to the left. When the donkey saw the angel of the LORD, it lay down under Balaam, and he was angry and beat it with his staff. "Then the LORD opened the donkey's mouth, and it said to Balaam, 'What have I done to you to make you beat me these three times?'

"Balaam answered the donkey, 'You have made a fool of me! If only I had a sword in my hand, I would kill you right now.'

"The donkey said to Balaam, 'Am I not your own donkey, which you have always ridden, to this day? Have I been in the habit of doing this to you?'

" 'No,' he said.

"Then the LORD opened Balaam's eyes, and he saw the angel of the LORD standing in the road with his sword drawn. So he bowed low and fell facedown.

"The angel of the LORD asked him, 'Why have you beaten your donkey these three times? I have come here to oppose you because your path is a reckless one before me. The donkey saw me and turned away from me these three times. If it had not turned away, I would certainly have killed you by now, but I would have spared it.'

"Balaam said to the angel of the LORD, 'I have sinned. I did not realize you were standing in the road to oppose me. Now if you are displeased, I will go back' " (Numbers 22:21-35).

God not only knows when His animals are being mistreated, but speaks out against cruel treatment toward animals as well as praising those who treat their animals with kindness: "The righteous care for the needs of their animals, but the kindest acts of the wicked are cruel" (Proverbs 12:10, NIV).

3. God is always watching over you and He even has given you angles that watch over you: "See that you do not despise one of

54

these little ones [children]. For I tell you that their angels in heaven always see the face of my Father in heaven" (Matthew 18:10, NIV, clarification mine).

4. "Blessed are those [this means you] who mourn, for they will be comforted" (Matthew 5:4, NIV, clarification mine).

5. God not only watches over little girls and boys, but He is concerned with how animals are treated too. "The righteous care for the needs of their animals, but the kindest acts of the wicked are [only] cruel" (Proverbs 12:10, NIV, clarification mine).

6. "For every animal of the forest is mine, and [even all] the cattle on a thousand hills. I know every bird in the mountains, and the insects in the fields are mine" (Psalm 50:10-11, NIV, clarification mine).

"Are not two sparrows sold for a penny? Yet not one of them will fall to the ground outside your Father's care" (Matthew 10:29, NIV).

7. "The LORD is gracious and compassionate, slow to anger and rich in love. The LORD is good to all; He has compassion on all He has made" (Psalm 145:8-9, NIV).

"Cast all your anxiety [worry] on Him because He cares for you" (1 Peter 5:7, NIV, clarification mine).

8. "For the earnest expectation of the creature waits for the manifestation of the sons of God. For the creature was made subject to vanity (self-centered/corruption) not willingly, but by reason of Him who subjected the same in hope, because the creature itself also shall be delivered from the bondage of corruption into the glorious liberty of the children of God [at the

End of the Age when Jesus returns]" (Romans 8:19-21, KJV clarification mine).

NOTE: Many modern translations use the term "creation" instead of "creature." The original Greek word used is *Ktisis* (κτίσις), Strong's word 2937, which can mean several things, including "creation" or "creature," depending on its context. The problem with translating *ktisis* as "creation" is when looking at Romans 8 in context, creation includes the planets, moons, stars, asteroids rocks, mountains, streams, oceans and seas, as well as creatures, both animals and humans. If we were to go with "creation," as most other versions of the Bible do, we would have to include the entire universe, beginning with Alpha Centauri (some 4.22 light-years from Earth), which is the nearest star system to our own solar system. However, the universe is made up of gasses, fire (suns), planets and rocks, which are inanimate objects that have no life in them and therefore cannot think or possess emotions. The five passages in Romans 8 deals with hope and anticipation, which is something that a rock on Mars or the rings around Saturn, or any other star systems cannot do because they are inanimate entities, so they do not have the capacity to think or reason. Let's now look at the last two verses of Romans 8:

"For we know that the whole creation groans and travails in pain together until now" (Romans 8:22). Here the King James does use the word "creation," as opposed to "creature." In this verse, Paul is using poetic license for dramatic effect. We continue to the last verse:

"And not only they (ask yourself which makes more sense, creation or creatures), but ourselves also, which have the first fruits of the Spirit, even we ourselves groan within ourselves, waiting the adoption, to wit, the redemption of our body" (Romans 8:23, clarifications mine).

It would be good to point out here that it was Adam and Eve who sinned and, therefore, a need for a Savior of mankind was required for people. Because animals never sinned against God, they are not in need of a personal Savior; nevertheless, they are still subjected to life in an imperfect body and world. As a result, the animals also wait to share in man's deliverance as we saw in the passage above.

9. "He will wipe every tear from their eyes. There will be no more death or mourning or crying or pain, for the old order of things has passed away" (Revelation 21: 4, NIV).

10. The Prophet Ezekiel tells us about a strange event with strange creatures he witnessed in Heaven:

"In my thirtieth year, in the fourth month on the fifth day, while I was among the exiles by the Kebar River, the heavens were opened and I saw visions of God.

"On the fifth of the month—it was the fifth year of the exile of King Jehoiachin—the word of the LORD came to Ezekiel the priest, the son of Buzi, by the Kebar River in the land of the Babylonians. There the hand of the LORD was on him.

"I looked, and I saw a windstorm coming out of the north—an immense cloud with flashing lightning and surrounded by brilliant light. The center of the fire looked like glowing metal, and in the fire was what looked like four living creatures. In appearance their

57

form was human, but each of them had four faces and four wings. Their legs were straight; their feet were like those of a calf and gleamed like burnished bronze. Under their wings on their four sides they had human hands. All four of them had faces and wings, and the wings of one touched the wings of another. Each one went straight ahead; they did not turn as they moved.

Their faces looked like this: Each of the four had the face of a human being, and on the right side each had the face of a lion, and on the left the face of an ox; each also had the face of an eagle (Ezekiel 1:1-10, NIV).

There are also lots of horses in Heaven too, "The armies of heaven were following Him [Jesus], riding on white horses and dressed in fine linen, white and clean" (Revelation 19:14, NIV, clarification mine)

11. The Apostle John also tells us what he saw and heard in Heaven. "The first living creature was like a lion, the second was like an ox, the third had a face like a man, the fourth was like a flying eagle" (Revelation 4: 7, NIV).

John again tells us, "Then I heard every creature in heaven and on earth and under the earth and on the sea, and all that is in them, saying: 'To Him who sits on the throne and to the Lamb be praise and honor and glory and power, for ever and ever!' The four living creatures said, 'Amen,' and the elders fell down and worshiped" (Revelation 5:13-14, NIV).

12. "God made the wild animals according to their kinds, the livestock according to their kinds, and all the creatures that move along the ground according to their kinds. And God saw that it was good.

"Then God said, "Let us make mankind in our image, in our likeness, so that they may rule over the fish in the sea and the birds in the sky, over the livestock and all the wild animals, and over all the creatures that move along the ground" (Genesis 1:25-26, NIV).

"So the man gave names to all the livestock, the birds in the sky and all the wild animals" (Genesis 2:20a, NIV).

13. "Now the LORD God had planted a garden in the east, in Eden; and there he put the man he had formed" (Genesis 2:8, NIV).

14. "Then God said, 'I give you every seed-bearing plant on the face of the whole earth and every tree that has fruit with seed in it. They will be yours for food. And to all the beasts of the earth and all the birds in the sky and all the creatures that move along the ground—everything that has the breath of life in it—I give every green plant for food.' And it was so" (Genesis 1:29-30, NIV).

15. "See, I will create new heavens and a new earth. The former things will not be remembered, nor will they come to mind" (Isaiah 65:17, NIV).

"But in keeping with His promise we are looking forward to a new heaven and a new earth, where righteousness dwells" (2 Peter 3:13, NIV).

16. "The wolf will live with the lamb, the leopard will lie down with the goat, the calf and the lion and the yearling together; and a little child will lead them" (Isaiah 11:6, NIV).

17. "The infant will play near the cobra's den, and the young child will put its hand into the viper's nest. They will neither harm nor destroy on all my holy mountain, for the earth will be filled with the knowledge of the LORD as the waters cover the sea" (Isaiah 11:8-9, NIV).

18. "In His hand is the life of every creature and the breath of all mankind" (Job 12:10, NIV).

19. Because the creature [animal] itself also shall be delivered from the bondage of corruption into the glorious liberty of the children of God (Romans 8:21, KJV, clarifications mine).

Again we are reminded:

"The wolf will live with the lamb, the leopard will lie down with the goat, the calf and the lion and the yearling together; and a little child will lead them. The cow will feed with the bear, their young will lie down together, and the lion will eat straw like the ox. The infant will play near the cobra's den, and the young child will put its hand into the viper's nest. They will neither harm nor destroy on all my holy mountain, for the earth will be filled with the knowledge of the LORD as the waters cover the sea" (Isaiah 11:6-9, NIV).

20. Once again we are reminded:

"And God shall wipe away all tears from their eyes; and there shall be no more death, neither sorrow, nor crying, neither shall there be any more pain: for the former things are passed away" (Revelation 21:4, KJV)

21. The Apostle John reveals the marvelous sighting of thousands and thousands of animals that he saw in the very throne room of God:

"And I beheld, and I heard the voice of many angels round about the throne and the beasts and the elders: and the number of them was ten thousand times ten thousand and thousands of thousands" (Revelation 5:11, KJV).

22. "I also said to myself, 'As for humans, God tests them so that they may see that they are like the animals. Surely the fate of human beings is like that of the animals; the same fate awaits them both: As one dies, so dies the other. All have the same breath; humans have no advantage over animals ...'" (Ecclesiastes 3:18-19, NIV).

23. We now look at one of the most misquoted Scriptures used by pastors, creators of Christian television networks, founders of Christian Nouthetic Counseling and other highly respected theologians who suggest that animals do not go to Heaven because the Bible says, "the spirit of the beast goes down!" However, that is not what the Bible says at all. The passage they are using as their "proof text" is Ecclesiastes 3:21, which is not a definitive statement of fact, but rather it is a rhetorical question that, in this instance, requires an answer in the negative.

    The problem is that these august stalwarts of the faith leave out the first few words of this passage, which makes all the difference in the world as to what the passage is saying. The passage reads, "*Who knows if* the human spirit rises upward and if the spirit of the animal goes down into the earth?" (Ecclesiastes 3:21, NIV, emphasis added).   The answer must be, "No one can tell!" However, as we shall see in the next end note, there is an answer to Solomon's rhetorical question. Read on.

24. "..., and the spirit returns to God who gave it" (Ecclesiastes 12:7, NIV).

25. Martin Luther, William Hazlitt, trans. *Table Talk* (London: Fount Papers [Harper Collins] Publ., 1995), 361.

26. "Animals and Religion," in *The Universe, Celebrating Scotland*, September 12, 1993, p. III. A reprint from *The Ark* (London: Catholic Study Circle for Animal Welfare).

27. John Wesley, "The General Deliverance" in *Sermons on Several Occasions,* Vol. II (London: Wesleyan Conference Office, 1874).

28. Richard Newman. *Bless All Thy Creatures, Lord: Prayers for Animals*. (New York: Macmillan, 1982). Print. Prayers attributed to St. Basil the Great.

29. Saint Francis, Church Tradition. One of several sayings and prayers regarding animals attributed to St. Francis of Assisi.

ALL SCRIPTURES USED AS REFFERENCES WERE RESEARCHED IN THEIR ORIGINAL LANGUAGES IN ORDER TO ENSURE THE ACCURACY OF THEIR EXACT MEANINGS AND INTENT, WHICH IS REFLECTED BY THE PARTICULAR VERSIONS USED.

ABOUT THE AUTHOR

As a student of theology, Dr. J.P. Sloane has spent over 30 years doing biblical research, which enabled him to study and graduate from the following schools: Purdue University through a program sponsored by *The Indiana Council of Churches*, the Institute of Charismatic Studies at Oral Roberts University, the Moody Bible Institute, and the Institute of Jewish-Christian Studies. He earned a B.A., *Summa Cum Laude*, from the Master's University where he also studied at their IBEX campus in Israel. While at the Master's University, he earned an M.A. in Biblical Counseling. At Trinity Theological Seminary he earned a Doctorate of Ministry as well as a Ph.D., *With Distinction*, in Religious Studies.

Throughout the years, Dr. Sloane has appeared on *The 700 Club, The PTL Club, Lester Sumrall Today, Richard Roberts Live,* LeSea Broadcasting's *Harvest,* and Trinity Broadcasting Network's *Praise the Lord,* to name a few.

Publications that Dr. Sloane appears in include, "Who's Who in the World" and "Who's Who in America." He is also featured in the "Dictionary of International Biography" and "2000 Outstanding Intellectuals of the 21st Century" (Cambridge, England).